In the Desert

Written by Becca Heddle

Collins

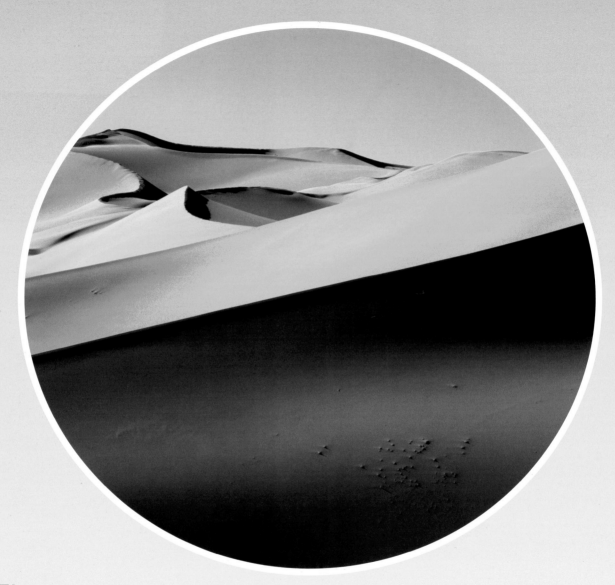

This is the desert.

3

There are flowers in the desert.

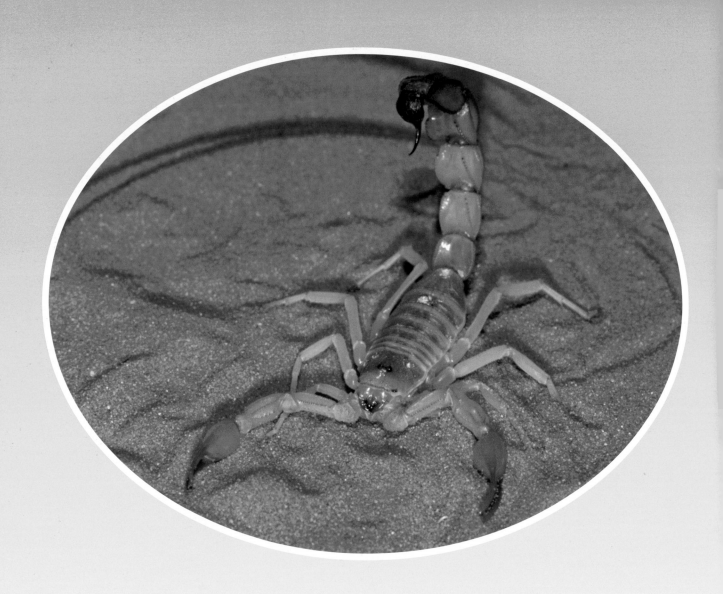

There are animals in the desert.

There are old cities in the desert.

There are new cities in the desert.

And there are children in the desert.

The desert

:paw: Ideas for guided reading :paw:

Learning objectives: use talk to organise, sequence and clarify thinking, ideas, feelings and events; read a range of familiar and common words and simple sentences independently; extend their vocabulary, exploring the meanings and sounds of new words; show an understanding of how information can be found in non-fiction texts to answer questions about where, who, why and how

Curriculum links: Knowledge and Understanding of the World: Find out about the environment, and talk about those features they like and dislike

High frequency words: this, is, the, are, in

Interest words: desert, flowers, animals, cities, children

Word count: 37

Resources: ICT, books about deserts, atlas or globe

Getting started

- Ask children to tell each other what they know about the desert. Prompt them with questions, e.g. *What is a desert? What is it like there? What lives in the desert?*

- Look at the front and back covers together. Discuss what can be seen in the pictures.

- Read the title and blurb aloud with the children, pointing to the words as you read.

- Ask children to predict what will be in the desert. Prompt them again, e.g. *Will there be buildings? Will there be flowers? What will they be like?* Make a list on the whiteboard.

Reading and responding

- Turn to p1. Ask children to tell a partner what they can see before sharing their ideas with the group.